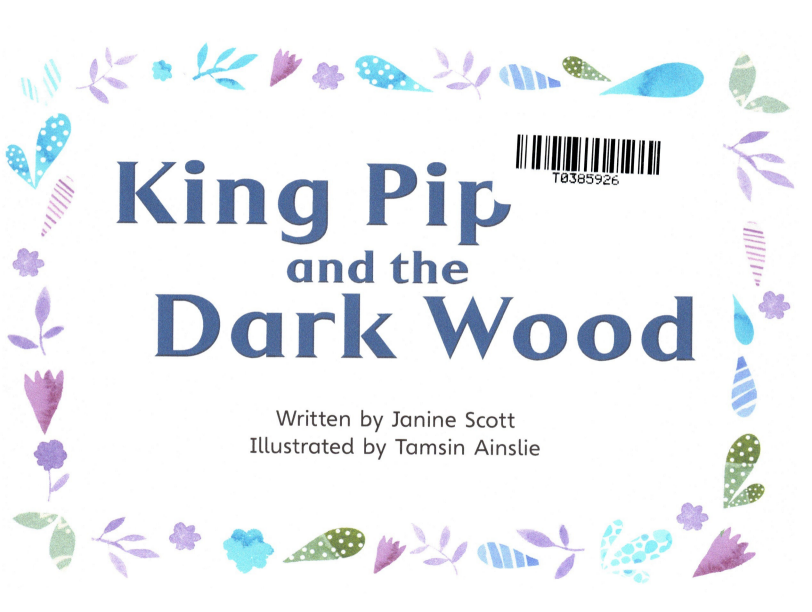

King Pip
and the
Dark Wood

Written by Janine Scott
Illustrated by Tamsin Ainslie

King Pip was in the wood.

He was lost. It got dark.

3

King Pip met an owl.

"Can you help me?
I am lost," he said.

"No," said the owl.

King Pip met a fox.

"Can you help me?" he said.

"No," said the fox.

King Pip met a rabbit.

"Can you help me?"
he said.

"No," said the rabbit.

q

"I need help!" said King Pip.
"Look, a bug!"

"I can help you,"
said the bug.

The bug had a light.

"Now I am not lost," said King Pip.